The 'homophob[ic']
free speech and religious liberty

Clause 126 of the Criminal Justice and Immigration Bill

First printed in January 2008

ISBN 978-1-901086-37-9

Published by The Christian Institute
Wilberforce House, 4 Park Road, Gosforth Business Park,
Newcastle upon Tyne, NE12 8DG

The Christian Institute is a Company Limited by Guarantee, registered in England as a charity.
Company No. 263 4440, Charity No. 100 4774.

Contents

Incitement to 'homophobic hatred'   5

Tragic cases   6

The existing law   7

Inadequate safeguards   11

A realistic concern   17

A climate of fear   19

A warning from Sweden   21

Tolerance is a two way street   22

Hateful lyrics in music   24

The Bishop of Chester case: 27
can you change sexual orientation?

"Temperate" language   29

The nature of religious discourse   32

Oversensitivity   34

Is this incitement law necessary?   35

Free speech amendment   37

References   39

Incitement to 'homophobic hatred'

Clause 126 of the Criminal Justice and Immigration Bill introduces a new offence of inciting hatred on grounds of sexual orientation. The Government has set the threshold of the proposed offence at "threatening" words or behaviour and requires proof of intention to stir up hatred. Although this reduces the scope for vexatious complaints, a wide-range of critics remain concerned about the implications for free speech. Prominent homosexual journalists and activists, such as Matthew Parris and Peter Tatchell, are among those to have voiced their opposition to the offence.

Of particular concern is the absence of a specific clause which explicitly protects free speech. Such a clause is present in the religious hatred offence. A cross-party free speech amendment to the 'homophobic hatred' offence, based on wording proposed jointly by the Church of England and the Roman Catholic Church, was debated in the House of Commons on 9 January 2008. It attracted 169 votes from all sides of the House. This tally could have been higher but for a separate Liberal Democrat amendment which also sought to amend the offence to protect free speech.

There is clearly wide-spread concern about 'hate speech' legislation and its impact on freedom of expression. This booklet sets out the concerns about the impact of a proposed 'homophobic hatred' law on free speech and religious liberty.

Tragic cases

Tragic cases do not necessarily justify specific laws. There have been many tragic murders of people who have a religious faith.

Since 1996 five Anglican or Roman Catholic clergy have been murdered,[1] with a Satanist recently being convicted for the latest of these crimes.[2] An academic study has found that 12% of clergy had experienced physical assault, with 70% experiencing some form of violence against them.[3] One in five had been threatened with harm. This has led to a suggestion from National Churchwatch that vicars should not wear their clerical collars in some non-church settings because it makes them vulnerable to attack.[4]

The Christian Institute does not believe that the way to tackle the assaults on church leaders is to clamp down on criticism of Christianity. We opposed the introduction of the incitement to religious hatred offence because of concerns over free speech. For the same reason we are against the proposed sexual orientation incitement offence.

As with the religious hatred law, evidence has been brought forward to justify a 'homophobic hatred' crime. Our view is that there is already adequate legislation to cover the kinds of cases that are being cited. And it is wrong to single out particular groups (such as religious people or homosexuals), leaving other groups (such as the elderly) with an inferior degree of protection.

The existing law

General

Under the criminal law, everyone is equally protected by existing laws against assault, murder and harassment. Public order offences outlaw threatening, abusive or insulting words or behaviour likely to cause harassment, alarm or distress. This is regardless of the background of either the culprit or the victim.[5]

Civil laws on defamation and those covering basic employment rights, such as unfair dismissal, also apply equally to all.

Specific offences protecting sexual orientation

Tougher sentences are given where a crime is found to have been aggravated by hostility on the grounds of sexual orientation.[6] There are also specific reporting procedures for 'homophobic incidents'. Sexual orientation is already specifically protected by regulations covering both employment[7] and the provision of goods and services.[8]

Legislation to replace incitement in the common law

In addition to all these laws above it is also unlawful under the common law to incite someone to commit a crime. These are called inchoate offences. Such incitement can be of a general nature, for example encouraging the assassination of political figures, despite impressions to the contrary given by Stonewall.[9]

In fact the Government has legislated to make it even easier to prosecute those who incite the commission of crime. Part 2 of the Serious Crime Act 2007, repeals the common law offence of inciting a crime. New laws against "encouraging or assisting" crime are introduced instead.

In the context of the present debate on gay hatred, the Prime Minister drew attention earlier this year to these planned changes to "...incitement law to make it easier to prove reckless encouragement of criminality".[10]

These broad new laws will clearly render unlawful appalling rap lyrics which incite violence against and the murder of homosexuals. The changes are based on Law Commission proposals. According to the Commission: "There should be no requirement that D has any particular individual(s) or group(s) as the target of his or her encouragement. If D posts a message on a web-site urging the assassination of all immigrants, he or she ought to be liable regardless of whether the encouragement is aimed at a particular individual, a group of individuals or the world at large."[11]

Horrendous examples of incitement to serious crime have been brought forward by Stonewall, yet the new laws on inchoate offences already address these concerns. Indeed, Home Office Minister Tony McNulty appears to have admitted that the new legislation could be used against rap lyrics which incite serious crime.[12]

Northern Ireland

Stonewall has cited the existing law in Northern Ireland against stirring up hatred based on sexual orientation as justification for introducing an equivalent law in Britain. Yet if Stonewall is concerned about rap music, why has it not sought to use the law in Northern Ireland, where such music is readily available? No complaint about lyrics made to incite 'homophobic hatred' has ever been received by the Police Service of Northern Ireland.[13]

Furthermore, just because a law exists in one religious and cultural situation does not mean it should be introduced in a different place. For example, the religious hatred law Parliament introduced in England and Wales is different to that which already existed in Northern Ireland, showing that the two jurisdictions can require different treatment because of their particular circumstances. The House of Lords Select Committee on Religious Offences in England and Wales discussed the transplanting of a law from one jurisdiction to another in their 2003 report. They concluded that, while it might be effective in the commercial sphere:

> "[s]uccessful transplant is more problematic where, as in the case of religiously related offences, they touch upon the mores and culture of a community."[14]

The same problem applies to an incitement to hatred law covering sexual orientation: there are clear cultural differences. The kinds of infringements of religious liberty that we have seen in England, such as the Roberts case, do not arise in Northern Ireland. The police in Northern Ireland, because of the community tensions that exist, are particularly concerned to protect free speech, which is one of the reasons why incitement to religious hatred is rarely prosecuted.[15]

Inciting crime and legitimate free speech

Peter Tatchell has written recently that laws against incitement to murder and incitement to violence should be used before seeking to create a new hate crime. He went on to raise serious concerns about free speech.[16]

There is crucial difference between inciting the commission of a crime and expressing an opposing view. Incitement to commit a crime, e.g. violence or murder, is rightly an offence and one which is made much broader by the changes included in the Serious Crime

Act. But the law must also protect freedom of speech, the right to express an opposing view – however strongly that view is expressed. The incitement to hatred offence sought by Stonewall violates the boundary. Such a law could be used to outlaw the expression of a legitimate opposing view.

Arguing against an incitement to *religious hatred law* in 2001, the Gay Times said:

> "The great danger of Mr Blunkett's new Act is that it would make it illegal to take issue with orthodox religious views of homosexuality."[17]

In other words, a law against incitement to religious hatred would have the effect of criminalising disagreement with "orthodox religious views". A parallel argument applies regarding an 'incitement to homophobic hatred' offence. To express the opinion that homosexual behaviour is morally wrong is to disagree with that particular lifestyle choice. It is not the same thing as hatred. There are real concerns that a 'homophobic hatred' offence will criminalise disagreement.

In the debates over the religious hatred law Parliament decided that protecting the free speech of millions of people must come before restricting even the insulting and abusive pronouncements of the BNP.

The Director of Liberty, Shami Chakrabarti sees an incitement to hatred offence as a further restriction on free speech:

> "What seems to me to be one of the dangerous by-products of so much legislation, so much authoritarian legislation in the last decade, is that we can become quite infantilised as a population, that we think that everything that isn't banned by criminal law equals sensitive, smart, good conduct. And what we should have is a space, a personal, ethical moral space that governs us before the criminal law governs us. And just because something is legal doesn't mean that it's a nice thing to say... But I do think that we could do with less anti-speech law in this country. For example, blasphemy, incitement to religious hatred, some overboard public order offences."[18]

Inadequate safeguards

The Christian Institute is often contacted by Christians who fear censure if they express their orthodox Christian beliefs on homosexuality. There are inadequate safeguards for religious liberties in the existing law. There already is a chilling effect.

Public Order Act 1986

The Public Order Act 1986 has been applied on some occasions in a way that it was never intended to be used. The most alarming case of injustice is that of the pensioner Harry Hammond, who suffered from Asperger's Syndrome, a form of autism. Sufferers can lack awareness of what is going on around them. When preaching in Bournemouth town centre, Mr Hammond held up a sign saying:

> "Stop Immorality", "Stop Homosexuality", "Stop Lesbianism", "Jesus is Lord".[19]

Mr Hammond was physically attacked by a group of protesters. Despite being forced to the ground and having mud and water thrown over him, it was Mr Hammond that was arrested, prosecuted and convicted under section 5 of the Public Order Act. One of the police officers on duty disagreed with his colleague over the arrest and he appeared as a witness for the defence.[20] Peter Tatchell has attacked Mr Hammond's conviction.[21]

The Hammond case is a disturbing precedent because it was a clear infringement of the right to free speech and freedom of religion. Mr Hammond was expressing the orthodox Christian belief that the practice of homosexuality is sinful, a belief which has since been recognised as being worthy of recognition under Article 9 of the European Convention on Human Rights.[22] The obvious concern is that, as Mr Hammond sharing his view on homosexuality was deemed to be committing a general public order offence, a specific sexual orientation incitement offence would be a further restriction on religious liberty. This would particularly be so if the wording of the offence mirrored the *racial hatred law* by covering "threatening, abusive or insulting words or behaviour". Section 5 of the Public Order Act uses these very same words, and yet Mr Hammond's sign was found to fall within this definition.

A heckler's veto

There is no doubt that it was only Harry Hammond who was physically assaulted, not any of the crowd listening to him. Yet the violent actions of the hearers were viewed as public disorder caused by Mr Hammond.

The law therefore creates an incentive for a heckler to riot, a heckler's veto. To stop someone you don't like you create a disturbance and have the speaker arrested.

An incitement to 'homophobic hatred' law would work in a similar way. Such a law creates an incentive for individuals to react strongly when criticised. The more offended the reaction, the more hateful the statement must surely have been.

Under the existing law, complaints to the police have already been used as a campaign tactic by some gay rights sympathisers. An incitement law will make matters far worse. It will encourage disharmony, rather than tolerance, between those with conflicting strong beliefs on sexual conduct.

Landlord Adrian Taylor was convicted under section 5 of the Public Order Act 1986 for a sign outside his pub that read "faggots and mince not on the menu". This was taken by the previous owners of the pub, a homosexual couple, as an insult against them, and a complaint was made to the police. The case ultimately resulted in a £500 fine.[23] If the criminal law can already censure comments at this level – essentially nothing more serious than a crude and tasteless joke – it has to be asked why a new incitement offence is thought necessary. Given the low threshold at which the Public Order Act is operating, what kind of statements do Stonewall envisage will be caught by an incitement offence which are not already covered by existing legislation?

The free speech threshold: religious vs racial incitement

The threshold for the incitement to religious hatred offence is much higher than the racial hatred offence because of three protections:

1. words or behaviour must be threatening;
2. abusive or insulting words or behaviour, instead of triggering the offence (as with race), are actually protected under a freedom of expression clause if they are made against a religion;[24]
3. intention to stir up hatred is required to commit the religious hatred offence, whilst the racial offence can be committed where hatred was "likely" to be stirred up by the words or conduct.

Thankfully, clause 107 (now 126) of the Criminal Justice and Immigration Bill, as inserted at Committee Stage in the Commons by the Government, includes two out of the three protections. Words or behaviour must be threatening before they are caught, and intention to stir up hatred must be proved.

However, the glaring omission is a free speech clause. The Government has not thought it necessary to mirror this part of the religious hatred law. This sends a signal to police and prosecutors that free speech is more important when considering a complaint under the religious hatred law than under the homophobic hatred law.

A homophobic incitement law even with robust safeguards for free speech would still have a massive chilling effect well beyond what the law says. This is best illustrated by considering the ACPO[25] hate incidents policy, in which the safeguards for religious liberty are plainly unsatisfactory.

Hate incident reporting procedure

The ACPO guidance describes a homophobic incident as:

> "Any incident which is perceived to be homophobic by the victim or any other person."[26]

The subjective emphasis of this definition, coupled with the pressure placed upon the authorities to respond to complaints, has caused significant problems. By emphasising the perception of the victim or any other person in defining something as an 'incident', regardless of the consideration of context or content that an objective evaluation could make, any semblance of legal reasonableness is stripped away.[27] The ACPO guidance actively encourages the police, on hearing a complaint, to confront individuals over their views on homosexuality, even when no crime has been committed.

Crown Prosecution Service

It has been suggested that the Crown Prosecution Service is a safeguard in that "they will only bring a case if there is a reasonable prospect of conviction and if a prosecution would be in the public interest".[28] However, given the CPS's definition of what constitutes 'homophobia' this is not reassuring. According to CPS guidance:

> "'Homophobia' and 'transphobia' are terms used to describe a dislike of LGBT people or aspects of their perceived lifestyle. In other words, homophobia and transphobia are not restricted to a dislike of individuals; the dislike can be based on any sexual act or characteristic that the person

associates with a LGBT person, whether or not any specific LGBT person does that act or has that characteristic. That dislike does not have to be so severe as hatred. It is enough that people do something or abstain from doing something because they do not like LGBT people."[29]

This definition shows that in the view of the CPS homophobia does not involve hating people, but can be simply the dislike of a particular sexual act. Saying that a particular sexual act is sinful would no doubt fall within this definition. This very low threshold for 'homophobia' raises serious concerns as to how effective a safeguard the CPS could be.

Attorney General

It is true that, assuming the new offence follows the pattern of existing incitement to hatred offences as a Parliamentary Labour Party briefing suggests, a prosecution will only be possible with the consent of the Attorney General.[30] However, the Attorney General cannot stop police investigating or arresting people for religious debate. He cannot stop them passing a file to the Crown Prosecution Service. He can only stop a prosecution. By that time the damage will have been done. Furthermore, the Attorney General and judges should not be required to adjudicate on people's personal opinions and religious beliefs.

There is also the issue of impartiality. During a debate on incitement to religious hatred during the passage of the Serious Organised Crime and Police Bill, the Rt Hon David Davis MP said:

> "The Government may say that the Bill states that cases will have to be approved by the Attorney-General, but does the Home Secretary not understand that in the highly politicised environment in which the decision to prosecute will have been made, the impartiality of the Attorney-General will be undermined?"[31]

The issue of impartiality is one of those at the heart of the current Government consultation on the role of the Attorney General. As the consultation document states: "some believe that the Attorney General cannot truly be (or be seen to be) independent from the Government (or party)"[32] and "concerns have been expressed about the Attorney General's role in relation to decisions about individual criminal cases".[33] The House of Commons Constitutional Affairs Committee has said that the situation is "not sustainable"[34] and recommended that the Attorney General should not be a party-political appointment.[35] The Attorney General cannot be considered a reliable safeguard when there is such uncertainty about the future nature of the post.

A realistic concern

Are the concerns about free speech realistic? Is there any evidence that such a law would be used to interfere with religious liberty? In recent years there has been a number of cases where police officers have investigated individuals because they made critical comments regarding homosexual practice. In many cases, these have been dealt with as 'hate incidents'.

In 2005 a Christian couple, Joe and Helen Roberts, were interrogated by police because they complained about their local council's 'gay rights' policy. The police said they were responding to a reported 'homophobic incident'. The police later admitted that no crime had been committed and, following legal action by the Roberts, the police and council issued a public apology.[36]

The Bishop of Chester was investigated by the Cheshire constabulary in November 2003 after he told his local newspaper of research showing that some homosexuals re-orientated to heterosexuality (see p.27). The police passed a file to the Crown Prosecution Service who decided not to prosecute. A statement issued by Cheshire Constabulary said, "The Crown Prosecution Service has been consulted with at length, and Cheshire Police are satisfied that no criminal offences have been committed, as current public order legislation does not provide specific offences based on sexuality."

In 2006 a Member of the Scottish Parliament asked Strathclyde Police to investigate remarks made by the Roman Catholic Archbishop of Glasgow. The Archbishop had defended the institution of marriage and criticised civil partnerships in a church service.

In 2004 the Christian Union of the University of Cambridge was reported to the police following its distribution of St John's gospel to students and hosting an evangelistic meeting where the Dean of Sydney Cathedral put forward "a traditional biblical view on homosexuality".

In December 2005 police questioned the family-values campaigner, Lynette Burrows, after she expressed the view on a radio programme that homosexual men may not be suitable for raising children. Police telephoned saying they were investigating a reported 'homophobic' incident.

The concept of 'hate incidents' and their impact on police practice has been analysed by constitutional lawyer and former Parliamentary Counsel, Francis Bennion. His article begins:

> "When is a law not a law? When it's made by the police. It looks like a law. It's enforced like a law. But it's not a law."[37]

He considers the examples of the Roberts, Sir Iqbal Sacranie (see below) and Lynette Burrows as cases where the definition of homophobic incidents has led to overzealous police action. Bennion describes it as police harassment. That these scenarios already take place raises the concern that the introduction of such an offence can only make matters far worse.

Given the number of cases which have been briefly referred to it does not seem unreasonable to fear that an incitement offence will be an even more powerful tactic to silence those who preach orthodox religious views on homosexual practice.

A climate of fear

One consequence of the current raft of legislation outlawing discrimination on grounds of sexual orientation is that it has created a climate of fear. So much so that a recent official enquiry concluded that one social work department failed to adequately investigate allegations of child abuse involving homosexuals for fear of being labelled 'homophobic'.

Social workers at Wakefield Council missed signs that Ian Wathey and Craig Faunch were abusing boys placed in their care between 2003 and 2005. An inquiry report into the case, published in August 2007 states: "The fear of being seen as prejudiced, the risk of talking about the words gay and paedophile together, was too great. There was a pervasive anxiety that, if this view was put forward in writing or verbally, the person putting it forward would be accused of being prejudiced and homophobic."[38]

Another staff member said: "You don't want to reflect negatively on gay couples, especially in social services. I'd be thinking 'am I being prejudiced, is it my own prejudice making me doubt the skills of these carers, these two gay men, is it because I'm homophobic?', rather than just asking the simple question 'are they abusing kids?'."[39]

Similarly, the official enquiry into the Islington child abuse scandal of the 1980s and 1990s found that investigations into homosexuals were blocked for politically-correct reasons. The report of the enquiry, the 'White Report', was strongly critical of the Council's application of equal opportunities policies to the detriment of child welfare.[40]

If social workers in these cases felt nervous about investigating homosexuals for fear of being labelled 'homophobic', it is in no way far-fetched to say that religious people will feel greatly intimidated by the presence of an incitement offence.

The depth of concern that religious people have regarding the proposed new offence was reflected in the joint memorandum submitted by the Church of England and Roman Catholic Bishops to the Public Bill Committee considering the Criminal Justice and Immigration Bill.[41]

A warning from Sweden

A similar law to the proposed incitement offence was introduced in Sweden in 2003. The Swedish law banned 'agitation' against homosexuals. When it was being proposed, Christians in Sweden were concerned that it could interfere with their freedom to express their religious belief that homosexual practice was sinful. But politicians assured them that in no way was the law intended to act in that way. The law was passed without specific protections for free speech and religious liberty.

Within the year a Christian minister was being prosecuted because he preached a sermon in his church in which he said homosexual practice was wrong. The case was pursued by the police and prosecuting authorities at the insistence of a local homosexual activist. The original trial found Pastor Ake Green guilty and sentenced him to one month in prison. Pastor Green had to fight all the way to the Swedish Supreme Court to clear his name. He succeeded because of European Convention rights to free speech and religious liberty.[42]

The reality is, once a law like this is on the statute book, pressure will be brought to bear to prosecute public statements of opposition to homosexual practice. Given recent high-profile police investigations into 'homophobic incidents', it is not unreasonable for Christians and those of other faiths to think that free speech and religious liberty will be unjustly interfered with under an incitement law.

Tolerance is a two way street

Roman Catholics have been labelled as being worse than paedophiles by eminent atheists. The BNP has similarly branded all homosexuals paedophiles. Both comments are untrue and felt to be deeply offensive, but why should it be legally permitted in one case, but not the other?

Christians are routinely called Nazis, lunatics, and much worse. People in the public eye say in all seriousness that religion should be banned. Charities even exist which campaign for society to be free from religion (Eg the *British Humanist Association* - charity no. 285987).

No one attempts to silence this criticism.

Religious believers have to have a thick skin.

Richard Dawkins in his book *The God Delusion* sets out a sustained argument that Roman Catholic priests are worse than paedophiles.

He states that "a significant proportion of the male population" of Ireland have as children suffered "legendary" brutality at the hands of Roman Catholic "Christian brothers". The same thing is claimed about school girls at the hands of the "often sadistically cruel nuns".[43]

Dawkins then goes on to say that the sexual abuse of children by priests "was arguably less than the long-term psychological damage inflicted by bringing the child up Catholic in the first place".[44]

In similar vein Dawkins attacks Protestants for teaching creationism in schools. They too are guilty of the mental abuse of children. Harry Hammond held up a sign saying "stop homosexuality". But similar sentiments are expressed about religion all the time. For example, Elton John recently said:

> "From my point of view I would ban religion completely. Organised religion doesn't seem to work. It turns people into really hateful lemmings and it's not really compassionate."[45]

Peter Tatchell compares Christians to Nazis for their 'crimes' against gays:

> "The Bible is to gays what Mein Kampf is to Jews. It is the theory and practice of Homo Holocaust."[46]

Hateful lyrics in music

Some heavy metal rock music includes extreme, blood-thirsty lyrics which call for Christians to be murdered. Here is one example from the track "Kill the Christian" from the album *Once upon the Cross* by Deicide (which is available to buy in the UK from Amazon.co.uk):

> You are the one we despise
> Day in day out your words compromise lives
> I will love watching you die
> Soon it will be and by your own demise...
>
> ... Satan wants you dead
> Kill the christian, kill the christian...
>
> ... Armies of darkness unite
> Destroy their temples and churches with fire...
>
> ... Kill the christian
> Kill the christian...dead!

Stonewall rightly protests about rap music which advocates killing homosexuals. The truth is that there are similarly murderous lyrics written about Christians or women. Rap music is also riddled with racism.

We certainly agree that some music is so dangerous that it should be banned. We believe that the Serious Crime Act renders this music unlawful. If this does not happen then the right approach may well be to have a certification procedure in the same way that we have for films, DVDs and, increasingly, computer games. There is still a level of censorship with films, DVDs and games, albeit at a very high level.

The rap lyrics quoted by Stonewall are abhorrent. But homosexuals are by no means the only targets of music. Other lyrics are racist, sexist, anti-Semitic and anti-Christian. For example:

Artist: Menace Clan
Album: Da Hood
Year: 1995
Title: Kill Whitey

> Niggas in the church say: kill whitey all night long...
> the white man is the devil... the CRIPS and Bloods are
> soldiers I'm recruiting with no dispute; drive-by shooting on this
> white genetic mutant... let's go and kill some rednecks...
> Menace Clan ain't afraid... I got the .380; the homies think I'm
> crazy because I shot a white baby; I said; I said; I said: kill
> whitey all night long... a nigga dumping on your white ass; fuck
> this rap shit, nigga, I'm gonna blast... I beat a white boy to
> the motherfucking ground.

Artist: Plan B
Album: Who Needs Actions When You Got Words
Year: 2006
Title: Kidz

> If I see something I want, then I'll take it, girl wont give it up,
> then I'll rape it, break it, inpenetrate it, I'm gonna make it happen,
> impregnate it, if she has a Jew I act like it aint mine, make her have
> an abortion for the 8th time.

Artist: Ice Cube
Album: Death Certificate
Year: 1991
Title: No Vaseline

...cuz you let a Jew break up my crew....
Cuz you can't be the Nigga 4 Life crew
with a white Jew tellin' you what to do.

Artist: Grief Of Emerald
Album: Christian Termination
Year: 2002
Title: Christian Termination

Christian termination
Christian termination
Cut their throats one by one
Christian termination has begun

The Bishop of Chester case: can you change sexual orientation?

The orthodox Christian view is that all sex outside of marriage is wrong. A homosexual inclination is not wrong, but homosexual practice is.

The clash between modern liberal views and Christianity is not just over sexual practice, but also over whether it is possible to change sexual orientation.

Even in gay circles there is a debate as to whether people can change their sexual orientation. Peter Tatchell has described the gay gene theory as "obviously a totally implausible theory". He continued, "it *is* a choice, and we should be glad it's that way and celebrate it for ourselves".[47]

In 2003 Professor Robert Spitzer published a study demonstrating that many of those in his study had changed their sexual orientation.[48] Professor Spitzer is a leading supporter of gay rights.[49]

In the week when the study was published the Bishop of Chester quoted Spitzer's conclusions that people can reorientate from homosexuality to heterosexuality. The Bishop was simply participating in the debate, yet a complaint led to a police investigation and even a file being passed to the Crown Prosecution Service. This was without an incitement law existing.

In such a controversial area, legislating for incitement on the grounds of sexual orientation risks unjustifiably silencing one side of the 'gay gene' argument. In response to the Spitzer research even pro-gay academics now accept that there can be "true change in core sexual orientation".[50]

"Temperate" language

Ben Summerskill from Stonewall is one of the main proponents of a homosexual incitement offence. He believes that an incitement offence would allow religious beliefs about homosexuality to be stated provided they were expressed in a temperate way.[51]

Strong language

The Old Testament describes spiritualism, cross-dressing, and homosexual practice as "an abomination".[52] Roman Catholic teaching describes homosexual practice as "an intrinsic moral evil; and thus the inclination itself must be seen as an objective disorder."[53]

'Perversion'

The late Cardinal Winning, former head of the Roman Catholic Church in Scotland, said of homosexuality:

> "I hesitate to use the word 'perversion', but let's face up to the truth of this situation, that's what it is. Are we now being asked to say what was wrong before is now right, and they can go ahead and do it?"[54]

The Cardinal made his remarks in the context of a debate about the repeal of Section 28, the law which banned the promotion of homosexuality in schools. If Stonewall succeeds in getting its law onto the statute book, a cardinal would face prosecution for saying something similar. This is a reasonable conclusion since Ben Summerskill has openly admitted that he wants an incitement law to criminalise statements of opinion such as one given by a protester outside Parliament in January 2007. Mr Summerskill heard someone shouting:

"Don't allow homosexuals to pervert these children".[55]

Mr Summerskill stated in oral evidence before the committee that this was "almost certainly incitement".[56] He has said that he was shocked that the Metropolitan Police permitted this particular Christian protest outside Parliament on 8 January 2007.[57]

The protest coincided with a House of Lords debate on whether to pass the Equality Act (Sexual Orientation) Regulations (Northern Ireland) 2006. Like Cardinal Winning the protesters were concerned about the promotion of homosexuality in schools. They were also concerned that the Regulations established a harassment law which restricted free speech. Subsequently the protesters' concerns were accepted by the Belfast High Court which quashed the controversial harassment provisions and ruled that the Regulations did not apply to the curriculum (rectifying statements made by Government ministers).

Mr Summerskill believes a homosexual incitement law is necessary because of statements by the BNP to the effect that gays are paedophiles.[58] Perhaps he interprets the word "pervert" as referring to paedophilia. However the context of the Christian protest was clearly about the promotion of homosexuality in the school curriculum and in society more generally. In the English Dictionary the word "pervert" means: "1 turn (a person or thing) aside from its proper use or nature. 2 misapply (words etc). 3 lead astray from right conduct or (esp. religious) beliefs; corrupt".[59]

Whatever the case, this serves to illustrate how misinterpretation of meaning could lead to accusations of incitement when in fact no offence is even close to being committed. Mr Summerskill made it clear that he was comfortable with leaving the determination as to whether or not incitement has taken place to a jury.[60] This seems a rather blasé and reckless approach to legislating in such a controversial area and enhances the concerns expressed above regarding the chilling effect. It is dangerous to create a law under which people will not know where they stand until they are actually in court.

The Government's clause 126 sets the threshold of the homophobic incitement law at "threatening" words or behaviour and requires proof of intention to stir up hatred. This reduces the scope for prosecutions but it does not explicitly direct prosecutors and the police to have regard to the legitimate exercise of free speech and religious liberty.

Even if there are no prosecutions (which is unlikely), the very existence of the law will make people fearful of expressing their views on this issue. This is the chilling effect on freedom of speech. Before a judge ever gets to hear a case under the new law, individuals will be making assessments of whether they feel their actions might fall foul of it and may well self-censor what they say as a result. The threat of police investigation can have a disproportionate effect on normally law abiding citizens and discourage them from coming anywhere near to crossing the line. As part of its Christian heritage, Britain has a long tradition of free speech. A homophobic incitement law runs counter to that. The criminal law should not be used as a political tool to silence opponents.

The nature of religious discourse

The expression of sincerely-held, mainstream religious beliefs may necessarily involve strong statements about moral conduct and eternal consequences. This is the nature of religious discourse. It is no less true when debating religious beliefs on sexual ethics. For example, the current Pope (when he was still a Cardinal) has said:

> "Although the particular inclination of the homosexual person is not a sin, it is a more or less strong tendency ordered toward an intrinsic moral evil; and thus the inclination itself must be seen as an objective disorder."[61]

The Bible itself contains strong statements about the eternal consequences of unrepentant sinful conduct. It speaks of hell for those who have not repented and trusted in Christ for the forgiveness of their sins, which includes – amongst many things – unrepentant immoral sexual practice.

The Bible's clear statements on the sinfulness of homosexual practice mean that those who hold to its teaching must believe that homosexual practice is wrong. As part of living out their faith as a witness for Jesus Christ, they will wish to state that certain activities are condemned by Scripture. Homosexual practice is one such activity. John Stott, a leading evangelical, has written the following:

> "The reason for the biblical prohibition [of homosexual practice] is the same reason why modern loving homosexual partnerships must also

be condemned, namely that they are incompatible with God's created order."[62]

"…the love-quality of gay relationships is not sufficient to justify them. Indeed, I have to add that they are incompatible with true love because they are incompatible with God's law."[63]

Nicky Gumbel, who runs the Alpha course, has said the Bible makes it clear that gay people need to be healed.[64]

Research by Minority Ethnic Christian Affairs has found that 98% of black church leaders in this country believe homosexuality to be a sin.[65]

It is not only the Bible which teaches that homosexual practice is morally wrong. Similar views are held by other religions, including orthodox Judaism, Islam, Sikhism and Baha'i. Consequently, it is not only Christians who make public statements giving their view.

Sir Iqbal Sacranie, former head of the Muslim Council of Britain, has said that homosexuality is "harmful" and "not acceptable".[66] In 2000, the Muslim Council of Britain issued a news release on the subject of section 28, stating the belief that "homosexual practices are morally wrong" and that "any teaching in schools which presents homosexual practices as equivalent to marriage or in a morally neutral way is profoundly offensive and totally unacceptable".[67]

No doubt references to hell and descriptions such as "intrinsic moral evil", "objective disorder", "sin", "incompatible with true love", "not acceptable" or "harmful" will be deeply insulting to many. Yet phrases like these do form part of mainstream religious discourse. Given that this is the case, there is genuine concern that an incitement offence would have a disproportionate impact on free speech where the expression of a religious belief is involved. A new incitement offence raises the prospect of police investigations into the statements of mainstream religious leaders.

Oversensitivity

Stonewall has published a report entitled 'Tuned Out', investigating the portrayal of lesbian and gay people on the BBC.[68] Stonewall cites "negative references" to, or stereotypes of, lesbian and gay people in The Lenny Henry Show, Porridge, The Weakest Link, A Question of Sport, Dead Ringers, Top Gear and other shows. For example, Anne Robinson's comment to a celebrity chef contestant on The Weakest Link, "What do you do in your restaurant? Just mince around?" is said to exhibit homophobia on the BBC.[69] The report shows the enormous range of programmes that Stonewall objects to and raises concerns as to how many of these they would consider ought to be outlawed by a new incitement law. It illustrates the low threshold at which gay rights activists start objecting to speech, even when what is said is obviously meant humorously. The fears raised regarding an incitement offence are clearly justified when those who will be complaining under the offence take umbrage so readily.

Is this incitement law necessary?

Homosexuals can be found at all levels of public life. Gay entertainers can be amongst the most popular people in Britain. The general population (including Christians) do not hate homosexuals. They treat them as any other member of society, though that doesn't mean that they approve of homosexual practice.

A leading liberal journalist has argued that gay rights are more advanced than racial rights. The Guardian's Jonathan Freedland (who is strongly pro-gay rights) has written on the heavy-handed actions of the police against people who disagree with homosexuality. He comments:

> "There are several intriguing elements here. One is the way the principle of gay rights has become so established that to oppose it is to guarantee one's ostracism from mainstream society: even the police have fully signed up. For this gay campaigners deserve enormous credit; it is one of the great political success stories of our time, for it now occupies a space that racial equality has struggled to reach." [70]

Rap artists and the BNP take pot shots at many groups, not just homosexuals. Tolerance is a two way street. If we want freedom of speech then we have to grant that right to others, even to say things which we find repellent. Any material which is threatening or which incites violence against anyone is a proper matter for the criminal law. Short of this the law does not exist to prevent people being offended.

As comedian Rowan Atkinson wrote in a letter to *The Times* lamenting the "sad futility" of an "unnecessary" law:

> "This 'tick the box if you'd like a law to stop people being rude about you' is one way of filling the legislative programme, but there are serious implications for freedom of speech, humour and creative expression… the casual ease with which some people move from finding something offensive to wishing to declare it criminal — and are then able to find factions within government to aid their ambitions — is truly depressing."[71]

Even prominent homosexuals say there is no need for the new law. The gay journalist Matthew Parris comments:

> "Lines of absolute principle are hard to draw, but some groups may be so weak and fragile as to need the law's protection from hateful speech. I'd like to think we gays are no longer among them."[72]

Free speech amendment debated in the Commons

The joint memorandum by the Church of England and Roman Catholic Bishops, already referred to above (p.20), raised similar concerns to our own regarding the chilling effect that a 'homophobic hatred' offence would have on free speech. On 9 January 2008, MPs debated Amendment 1, a cross-party amendment based on a draft in the memorandum, which sought to counter this chilling effect by placing on the face of the legislation a protection for freedom of speech.[73] It would have required police and prosecutors to have regard for freedom of speech before pursuing a complaint, just as they do under the religious hatred law. Amendment 1 would have introduced a new section 29JA into the Public Order Act 1986 similar to section 29J which was inserted by the Racial and Religious Hatred Act 2006. However, 29JA is less far-reaching than 29J. The terms "dislike, ridicule, insult or abuse" were removed (as shown on the next page). The amendment was defeated by 338 votes to 169.

Homophobic hatred offence Amendment 1 : free speech clause debated in the Commons, 9 January	Religious hatred offence Free speech clause
Proposed 29JA "Nothing in this Part shall be read or given effect in a way which prohibits or restricts discussion of, criticism of or expressions of antipathy towards, conduct relating to a particular sexual orientation, or urging persons of a particular sexual orientation to refrain from or modify conduct related to that orientation."	29J "Nothing in this Part shall be read or given effect in a way which prohibits or restricts discussion, criticism or expressions of antipathy, dislike, ridicule, insult or abuse of particular religions or the beliefs or practices of their adherents, or of any other belief system or the beliefs or practices of its adherents, or proselytising or urging adherents of a different religion or belief system to cease practising their religion or belief system."

References

1. *The Guardian*, 8 October 2007
2. *The Times*, 17 October 2007; *The Independent*, 17 October 2007
3. 'Violence Against Professionals in the Community Study – The Accounts and Experiences of Anglican Clergy', Economic and Social Research Council, July 2001
4. Tolson, N, *The Clergy Lifestyle Theory*, 2007, para. 2.4
5. Public Order Act 1986, Section 5
6. Criminal Justice Act 2003, Section 146
7. Employment Equality (Sexual Orientation) Regulations 2003
8. Equality Act (Sexual Orientation) Regulations 2007
9. *Inchoate Liability for Assisting or Encouraging Crime*, The Law Commission, No. 300, July 2006, para. 3.22, and Select Committee on Religious Offences in England and Wales, Session 2002-03, HL Paper 95-I, vol. 1, para.70 cf: House of Commons Public Bill Committee – Criminal Justice and Immigration Bill, Hansard, Second Sitting, 16 October 2007 (Afternoon), col. 79
10. *Pinknews.co.uk*, 17 July 2007
11. *Inchoate Liability for Assisting or Encouraging Crime*, Op cit, para. 5.52
12. House of Commons, Hansard, 22 October 2007, cols 118-119
13. House of Commons, Hansard, 29 October 2007, col. 607 wa
14. Select Committee on Religious Offences in England and Wales, Session 2002-03, HL Paper 95-I, vol. 1, Appendix 5, para. 1
15. Select Committee on Religious Offences in England and Wales, Session 2002-03, HL Paper 95-I, vol. 1, Appendix 5, para. 4
16. *Guardian Online*, 10 October 2007
17. *Gay Times*, November 2001
18. *The House Magazine*, 8 October 2007
19. Ahdar, R and Leigh, I, *Religious Freedom in the Liberal State*, OUP, 2005
20. *The Mail on Sunday*, 5 May 2002
21. *The Mail on Sunday*, 26 May 2002
22. The Christian Institute & Ors, Re Application for Judicial Review [2007] NIQB 66, para. 50
23. *Western Daily Press*, 19 October 2007
24. Public Order Act 1986, Section 29J
25. The Association of Chief Police Officers
26. 'Delivering a Quality Service: Good Practice and Tactical Guidance', Home Office Police Standards Unit and the Association of Chief Police Officers, March 2005, page 11
27. See Bennion, F, 'New Police Law Abolishes the Reasonable Man (and Woman)', *Justice of the Peace*, 170, January 2006, page 27
28. Parliamentary Labour Party briefing, 16 October 2007
29. *Guidance on Prosecuting Cases of Homophobic Crime*, Crown Prosecution Service, November 2002, page 3
30. Parliamentary Labour Party briefing, 16 October 2007
31. Serious Organised Crime and Police Bill, Second Reading, House of Commons, Hansard, 7 December 2004, col.1066
32. *The Governance of Britain: A Consultation on the Role of the Attorney General*, Attorney General's Office, July 2007, page 12
33. *The Governance of Britain: A Consultation on the Role of the Attorney General*, Attorney General's Office, July 2007, page 13
34. House of Commons Constitutional Affairs Committee, *Constitutional Role of the Attorney General*, Session 2006-7, HC 306, July 2007, page 23
35. House of Commons Constitutional Affairs Committee, *Constitutional Role of the Attorney General*, Session 2006-7, HC 306, July 2007, page 42
36. For supporting evidence on this and the subsequently mentioned cases, see: http://www.christian.org.uk/rel_liberties/cases/index.htm

37   Bennion, F, 'New Police Law Abolishes the Reasonable Man (and Woman)', *Justice of the Peace*, 170, January 2006, page 27

38   Independent Enquiry Report into the circumstances of Child Sexual Abuse by two Foster Carers in Wakefield, Wakefield Metropolitan District Council, August 2007, page 75, para. 9.232

39   *Ibid*, page 125, para. 9.537

40   *The Independent*, 24 May 1995; *The Observer*, 6 July 2003; *The Sunday Times*, 16 November 2003

41   Memorandum submitted by the Department for Christian Responsibility and Citizenship, Catholic Bishops' Conference of England and Wales, and the Mission & Public Affairs Council of the Church of England, see http://www.publications.parliament.uk/pa/cm200607/cmpublic/criminal/memos/ucm40302.htm as at 3 January 2007

42   See http://www.christian.org.uk/rel_liberties/cases/green_ake.htm

43   Dawkins, R, *The God Delusion*, Bantam Press, 2006, page 317

44   *Loc cit*

45   *Press Association National Newswire*, 11 November 2006

46   http://www.petertatchell.net/religion/2000.htm as at 19 October 2007

47   *The Observer*, 25 April 1999

48   Spitzer, R L, 'Can Some Gay Men and Lesbians Change Their Sexual Orientation? 200 Participants Reporting a Change from Homosexual to Heterosexual Orientation', *Archives of Sexual Behaviour*, 32(5), 2003, pages 403-417

49   His campaign led to the declassification of homosexuality as a psychiatric illness in the USA.

50   Wakefield, JC, 'Sexual Reorientation Therapy: Is It Ever Ethical? Can It Ever Change Sexual Orientation?' in *Ex-Gay Research: Analysing the Spitzer Study and Its Relation to Science, Religion, Politics, and Culture*, Drescher J and Zucker, K J (Eds), The Haworth Press, 2006

51   *Daily Mail*, 9 October 2007; House of Commons Public Bill Committee – Criminal Justice and Immigration Bill, Hansard, Second Sitting, 16 October 2007 (Afternoon), col. 76

52   Deuteronomy 18:9-12; 2 Kings 23:24; Deuteronomy 22:5; Leviticus 18:22 [Authorised Version]

53   *Letter to the Bishops of the Catholic Church on the pastoral care of homosexual persons*, Joseph Cardinal Ratzinger, section 3, 1 October 1986, see http://www.vatican.va/roman_curia/congregations/cfaith/documents/rc_con_cfaith_doc_19861001_homosexual-persons_en.html as at 19 October 2007

54   *'Winning Weighs In'*, BBC Frontline Scotland Programme 4 April 2000 see also http://news.bbc.co.uk/1/hi/scotland/701223.stm as at 19 October 2007

55   House of Commons Public Bill Committee – Criminal Justice and Immigration Bill, Hansard, Second Sitting, 16 October 2007 (Afternoon), col. 78

56   *Loc cit*

57   *Stonewall EBulletin*, 14 February 2007

58   House of Commons Public Bill Committee – Criminal Justice and Immigration Bill, Hansard, Second Sitting, 16 October 2007 (Afternoon), col. 75

59   Pocket Oxford Dictionary, OUP, 2000

60   House of Commons Public Bill Committee – Criminal Justice and Immigration Bill, Hansard, Second Sitting, 16 October 2007 (Afternoon), col. 84

61   Letter to the Bishops of the Catholic Church on the pastoral care of homosexual persons, *Op cit*

62   Stott, J, *Same Sex Partnerships? A Christian Contribution to Contemporary Debate*, Marshall Pickering, 1998, page 22

63   Stott, J, *Same Sex Partnerships? A Christian Contribution to Contemporary Debate*, Marshall Pickering, 1998, page 30

64   The Guardian, 'Catch me if you can', see http://www.guardian.co.uk/Archive/Article/0,4273,4078844,00.html as at 02 January 2008

65   Black Britain, 'Black church leaders welcome government ruling on same sex marriage denouncing homosexuality as a sin', 2 August 2006, see http://www.blackbritain.co.uk/news/details.aspx?i=2238&c=uk&h=Black+church+leaders+welcome+government+ruling+on+same+sex+marriage+denouncing+homosexuality+as+a+sin as at 7 November 2007

66   BBC News Online, 'Muslim head says gays 'harmful'', 3 January 2006, see http://news.bbc.co.uk/1/hi/uk/4579146.stm as at 6 November 2006

67   Muslim Council of Britain, Press Release, *Keep Clause 28 Grave Danger in Government Plans to Repeal Clause 28*, 26 January 2000

68   Cowan, K and Valentine, G, *Tuned Out: The BBC's portrayal of lesbian and gay people*, Stonewall, see http://www.stonewall.org.uk/documents/tuned_out_pdf.pdf as at 7 November 2007

69   Cowan, K and Valentine, G, *Tuned Out: The BBC's portrayal of lesbian and gay people*, Stonewall, see http://www.stonewall.org.uk/documents/tuned_out_pdf.pdf as at 7 November 2007, pages 8-9

70   *The Guardian* 18 January 2006

71   *The Times*, 7 November 2007

72   *The Times*, 11 October 2007

73   The amendment can be found towards the end of the memorandum.